WITH GRATITUDE

The 5 Minute Gratitude Journal

DAILY WRITING PROMPTS TO FOCUS ON THANKFULNESS

ISBN: 9798508851620

This journal belongs to:

___

"WHEN I STARTED COUNTING MY BLESSINGS,
MY WHOLE LIFE TURNED AROUND."

Willie Nelson

TODAY'S DATE ____ DAY 1

Who is the one family member you can always rely on? What makes that person so special?

Make that person's day by telling them how grateful you are for their presence in your life.

What's the biggest accomplishment in your personal life?

Don't be afraid to toot your own horn! You're worth it!

TODAY'S DATE ____ DAY 3

What's the biggest accomplishment in your professional life?

Be proud of your accomplishments! Your hard work paid off!

DAY 4 TODAY'S DATE ___

Think about your day. Write about one (or more!) things that brought you joy today.

Be grateful for the moments that make you smile!

TODAY'S DATE ____ DAY 5

Music can be therapeutic. Which musical artists or songs have brought you joy through the years?

Listen to your favorite music while journaling each day!

DAY 6 TODAY'S DATE ___

How did you help someone today? How did it make you feel to lend a helping hand?

"Always have a willing hand to help someone. You might be the only one that does." - Roy T. Bennett

TODAY'S DATE ____

What is your favorite sound in the world?
Why does it make you happy?

Surround yourself with sounds that soothe your soul.

DAY 8 TODAY'S DATE ___

Who is your favorite person in the world?
What makes them so special?

Call or send a text to let that person know how special they are.

TODAY'S DATE ____ DAY 9

Write about something that always cheers you up, no matter how bad of a day you're having.

Be thankful for the little things that bring you joy.

DAY 10 TODAY'S DATE ___

Write about a time when a random act of kindness (either given or received) made a difference in your life.

Try to do one good thing for someone each and every day!

TODAY'S DATE ____

What are your favorite hobbies? What do you love about it? Why is that activity special to you?

"The desire to create is one of the deepest yearnings of the human soul." - Dieter F. Uchtdorf

DAY 12 TODAY'S DATE ___

Think about your childhood and teenage years. Which experiences are you most grateful for? Why?

Be grateful for the experiences that turned you into the amazing person you are today!

TODAY'S DATE _____ DAY 13

Reading is a wonderful way to escape the real world.
Write about some of your favorite books.
What makes them special to you?

Take the time to read one chapter from your favorite book today!

DAY 14 TODAY'S DATE ___

Self-care is vital for our mental health.
How have you taken care of yourself today?

Your can't pour from an empty cup.
Take care of you, too.

TODAY'S DATE _____ DAY 15

Reading is a wonderful way to escape the real world.
Write about some of your favorite books.
What makes them special to you?

Take the time to read one chapter from your favorite book today!

DAY 16 TODAY'S DATE _____

Self-care is vital for our mental health.
How have you taken care of yourself today?

Your can't pour from an empty cup.
Take care of you, too.

TODAY'S DATE _____ DAY 17

Reading is a wonderful way to escape the real world.
Write about some of your favorite books.
What makes them special to you?

Take the time to read one chapter from your favorite book today!

DAY 18 TODAY'S DATE ______

A well-organized pantry? A warm bubble bath?
Talk about something in your home that brings you joy.

"The light is what guides you home,
The warmth is what keeps you there." - Ellie Rodriguez

TODAY'S DATE _____ DAY 19

Spending time in nature can be relaxing after a long, stressful week. When was the last time you enjoyed the beauty of the great outdoors?

"Heaven is under our feet as well as over our heads."
-Henry David Thoreau

What family tradition are you most thankful for?
Why is it so special to you?

"Family is not an important thing. It's everything."
-Michael J. Fox

TODAY'S DATE _____ DAY 21

Vacations can be restorative to the mind, body, and soul.
Write about your favorite vacation.
What made it so memorable?

"A vacation is having nothing to do and all day to do it in." - Robert Orben

DAY 22 TODAY'S DATE ___

They say laughter is the best medicine.
Write about something that made you laugh today.

Take some time today to watch your favorite comedy show or movie. Bonus points: Share that laugh with a friend!

TODAY'S DATE _____ DAY 23

Your job can be a source of stress, but if you look hard enough, you might just find some joy at work, too! What do you love about your job?

Do something nice for a co-worker today!

DAY 24 TODAY'S DATE ___

What is a hardship you experienced that had a silver lining?

"There's a crack in everything. That's how the light gets in."- Leonard Cohen

TODAY'S DATE ____ DAY 25

Pets can be a source of comfort and contentment. Talk about your pet and how the animal has made a difference in your life.

"Animals are such agreeable friends. They ask no questions. They pass no criticisms." - George Eliot

DAY 26 TODAY'S DATE ___

Self-love can be a hard concept, especially when it comes to the human body. Take a moment to reflect on the parts of your body you're most grateful for today.

"To love yourself right now, just as you are, is to give yourself heaven." - Alan Cohen

TODAY'S DATE ____ DAY 27

What's the hardest thing you've ever had to do? What made it so difficult? How did you feel once you survived it?

"So far, you've survived 100% of your worst days. You're doing great." - Norm Kelly

DAY 28 TODAY'S DATE ___

Holidays can be a source of joy (and stress). What's your favorite, stress-free holiday?

"Life starts all over again when it gets crisp in the fall."
-F. Scott Fitzgerald

TODAY'S DATE ____

Everyone has qualities and skills that makes them unique. What skills are easy for you that may not be so easy for others? How do you use those gifts?

Be proud of your gifts and use them to bring joy to yourself and others.

DAY 30 TODAY'S DATE ___

There's nothing like a supportive partner with which to share your hopes and dreams. Tell us about yours.

If you haven't found it yet, keep looking. Don't settle.
As with all matters of the heart,
you'll know when you find it. - Steve Jobs

TODAY'S DATE ____ 

Everyone has qualities and skills that makes them unique. What skills are easy for you that may not be so easy for others? How do you use those gifts?

Be proud of your gifts and use them to bring joy to yourself and others.

DAY 30 TODAY'S DATE ___

There's nothing like a supportive partner with which to share your hopes and dreams. Tell us about yours.

*If you haven't found it yet, keep looking. Don't settle.
As with all matters of the heart,
you'll know when you find it. - Steve Jobs*

TODAY'S DATE ____ DAY 31

You did it! You committed to one month of gratitude journaling! Be proud of yourself! What did you enjoy most about this experience?

Investing in yourself is the best investment of all.

About the Author

USA Today Bestselling Author Sydney Logan writes heartfelt romances that feature strong women and the men who love them. In addition to her novels, she has penned several short stories and is a contributor to Chicken Soup for the Soul. Just recently, she has released her first in a series of gratitude journals to motivate and encourage others to focus on contentment and joy.

She is a Netflix junkie, music lover, and a Vol for Life. Sydney and her husband make their home in beautiful East Tennessee.

To learn more about Sydney and her books, visit her online at sydneylogan.com.